BRUTALIST

LUXURY HOME CONCEPTS

VINSON

INTRODUCTION

Brutalist architecture stands as a defiant expression of form and function, a bold response to the intricacies of modern living. Born in the post-war era, this design movement strips away ornamentation and embraces the raw, the elemental, and the unadorned. In this collection, we journey through the evolution of brutalism as reimagined by the algorithmic genius of AI, combining modern luxury with the concrete bones of a style once misunderstood.

At the heart of brutalism lies a reverence for structure — exposed, unapologetic, and monumental. The buildings showcased in these pages are crafted from a palette of heavy, robust materials: rough-cast concrete, steel, and glass. Each home in this collection exudes an austere beauty, where texture becomes an expression of authenticity. The cool, tactile surfaces of poured concrete are contrasted by the sleekness of industrial glass, allowing light to penetrate the otherwise fortress-like facades. Steel frames lend a sense of precision, anchoring the design in modernity while maintaining the brutalist commitment to minimalism.

But brutalism is not simply about hardness. It is about creating dialogue between space and material, between the solid and the void. The interplay of shadow and light dances across rough textures, transforming these homes into living sculptures. The raw beauty of unfinished surfaces invites touch, while open spaces create a sense of freedom and clarity. This fusion of brutalist design principles with contemporary luxury makes these homes not just places to live, but works of art in their own right.

In this collection, we celebrate brutalism's rugged grandeur, reinvented through the lens of modern technology and creative vision. Welcome to the new era of brutalist luxury.

Printed in Great Britain
by Amazon

54044626R00059